AUSTRALIA'S REMARKABLE WILDLIFE

JOHN LESLEY

CASSOWARY

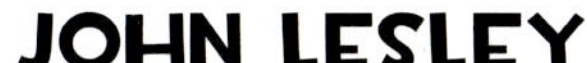

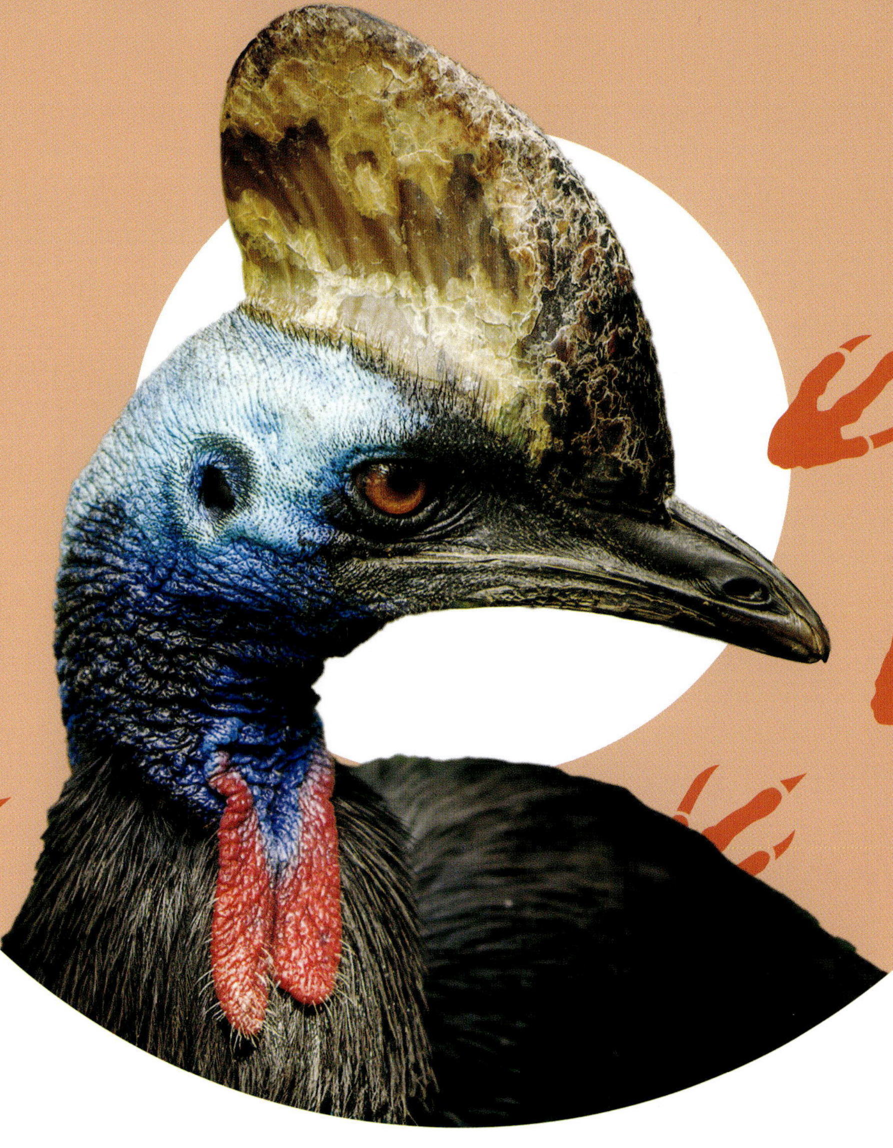

REDBACK publishing

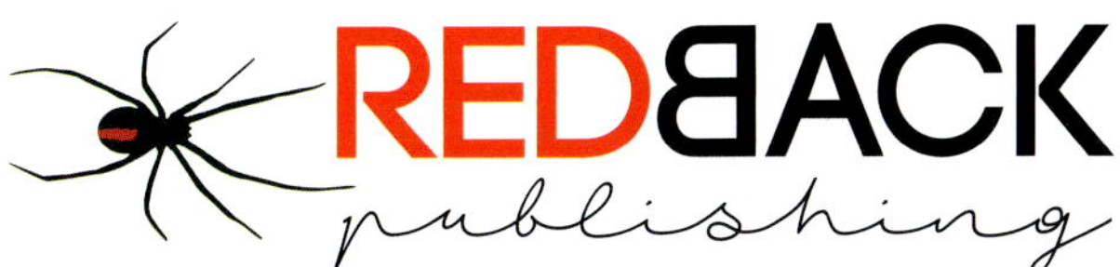

First Published 2025 by
Redback Publishing
Suite 6, 13a Narabang Way,
Belrose NSW 2085
Australia

www.redbackpublishing.com
info@redbackpublishing.com

ISBN 978-1-761401-32-9

Author: John Lesley
Editors: Lucinda Dodds and Emma Dobinson
Design: Redback Publishing

A catalogue record for this book is available from the National Library of Australia

Original illustrations © Redback Publishing 2025
Originated by Redback Publishing

Acknowledgements
Abbreviations: l—left, r—right, b—bottom, t—top, c—centre, m—middle
We would like to thank the following for permission to reproduce photographs: (Images © shutterstock)
p4-5c imageBROKER.com GmbH & Co. KG/Alamy Stock Photo, p4bl www.viajar24h.com, CC BY 2.0 <https://creativecommons.org/licenses/by/2.0>, via Wikimedia Commons, p4br Gaurav Nalkur, CC BY-SA 3.0 <https://creativecommons.org/licenses/by-sa/3.0>, via Wikimedia Commons, p7tl Henner Damke/Alamy Stock Photo, p26bl Judi Lapsley Miller, CC BY 4.0 <https://creativecommons.org/licenses/by/4.0>, via Wikimedia Commons, p14bl EarlyBird/Alamy Stock Photo, p20-21c Suzanne Long/Alamy Stock Photo, p21br Minden Pictures/Alamy Stock Photo, p29ml Santonius Santonius Silaban/Alamy Stock Photo, p32 Dave Watts/Alamy Stock Photo

CONTENTS

WHAT IS A CASSOWARY?

Cassowaries are flightless birds that are native to the rainforests of northern Queensland in Australia and parts of New Guinea. The southern cassowary stands at nearly two metres high and weighing as much as an adult human.

Southern cassowary

There are three species of cassowary alive today. The Australian southern cassowary lives in northern Queensland and southern New Guinea. The northern cassowary and the dwarf cassowary both live in the rainforests of New Guinea, and in some of the surrounding islands.

Northern cassowary

Dwarf cassowary

Some people think the cassowary is the living bird that most resembles the prehistoric, bird-like dinosaurs, due to its aggressive behaviour when it feels threatened.

It's hard to believe, but one of the cassowary's closest relatives is the little kiwi from New Zealand.

Little kiwi

CASSOWARY BASIC FACTS

SCIENTIFIC NAME

The scientific name of the southern cassowary of Australia is *Casuarius casuarius*.

SIZE & SHAPE

The female cassowary is larger and heavier than the male. They grow up to two metres tall, and an adult can weigh about 60 kilograms.

SOUNDS

Cassowaries make a variety of sounds. The loudest is a deep booming that they use to communicate with each other. The father makes a clicking noise with his beak to show the chicks the food they can eat.

The southern cassowary is the third biggest flightless bird in the world, after the ostrich (Africa) and the emu (Australia).

EYESIGHT

The cassowary has excellent close-up eyesight, a feature of birds that search for seeds and ripe fruit. The eyes are forward-pointing, which allows stereoscopic vision, a necessity for judging distance.

COLOUR

Feathers: : blue-black, long and thin

Eyes: dark orange

Neck and head: naked, with blue and red skin

Head: brown casque on top of the head

CONSERVATION STATUS

The International Union for Conservation of Nature (IUCN) Red List of Threatened Species says that the cassowary is VULNERABLE. This means that any major change in its habitat, availability of food, or difficulty in finding mates could lead to the threat of extinction.

In Australia, southern cassowaries are on the official list of endangered animals.

CASSOWARY BODY

The southern cassowary is an impressive-looking bird, with an aggressive attitude, an array of natural weaponry, and a reputation for being unpredictable in its behaviour towards people.

EARS

The cassowary's ears are holes on each side of its head. In other types of birds, these holes are covered by their feathers.

WATTLES

In birds, wattles are flaps of skin that hang down under the beak. They are often brightly coloured and are used for display to other birds. The southern cassowary has two long wattles that are pink or red.

FEATHERS AND SKIN

Like emus and ostriches, which are also unable to fly, cassowaries have a dense covering of long, fine feathers and a naked neck, but they are much more colourful.

THREAT DISPLAY

When they're feeling threatened, cassowaries will sometimes do a 'threat display' where they puff up their feathers, and make themselves look as big and scary as possible.

FEET AND CLAWS

Southern cassowaries have a big, heavy body and long, skinny legs with three toes on each foot. The inner toe on each foot is tipped with a long claw, like a dagger, that can grow to over 12 centimetres long. This weapon can inflict dreadful damage on a predator or a human who gets too close.

CASSOWARY CASQUE

The casque is a large, hard crest on top of the head. The cassowary is the only ratite bird that has a casque on its head. Each casque is unique, making it a feature used by biologists to identify individual birds they are studying.

Many dinosaurs had a bony growth on their heads just like the cassowary casque. Working out what it is for in living birds will help scientists understand their purpose in dinosaurs as well.

The reason a cassowary has evolved a casque is not known for certain, but here are a few of the ideas that biologists have for what its purpose might be:

- **Used to help the bird control its body temperature**
  - Birds are not warm-blooded like mammals, so they have different ways to control their body temperature.
- **Used for defence and fighting**
  - The shape of the casque might protect the head during a fight.
- **Used to help make the low, booming sound the cassowary uses to communicate**
  - The booming sound is so loud, a human can feel it as a vibration in their body.
- **Used to show other cassowaries the age and status of the bird**
  - The cassowary chicks hatch without a casque. It grows slowly, and its size may show other cassowaries the maturity of the bird.

The casque, along with the big, clawed feet, make the cassowary look like it might be a feathered dinosaur. It is not closely related to the dinosaurs it resembles, but all birds are descended from prehistoric dinosaur ancestors.

The outer part of the casque is made of keratin, which is the same substance that forms human finger nails.

CASSOWARY HABITAT

Southern cassowaries live in the rainforests of Northern Queensland and southern New Guinea, where they spend most of their time searching for food on the forest floor. The loss of forests through logging, bushfires, clearing and climate change is having a negative effect on the southern cassowary in Australia.

Cassowaries are important for the continued survival of the rainforest, since they spread the seeds of plants in their droppings, ensuring the survival of many native trees and bushes. Some of the rainforest plants have evolved to largely depend on the cassowary to spread the plant's seeds to other parts of the forest.

Cassowaries can swim, but they may drown in a heavy, tropical rainstorm. The chicks are particularly vulnerable when a cyclone lashes their habitat.

Its dense feathers provide protection against thorns and branches as the cassowary pushes its way through the thick growth on the forest floor.

CASSOWARY LIFECYCLE

LIFESPAN

Cassowaries may live for twenty years in the wild, and even longer in a zoo.

GROWING UP

As the chicks mature, there is a change in behaviour, and the father and chicks can become aggressive with each other. This is a natural behaviour that encourages the young birds to move away and claim other areas of the forest for themselves. It also prevents in-breeding amongst animals that are closely related.

CHICKS

The chicks will stay with their father until they are big and strong enough to take care of themselves. During this time, they learn where to find fruit and what to eat by following their father and watching what he does.

EGGS

The lifecycle of a cassowary starts with eggs that the female lays. The eggs are a dull green colour which provides them with camouflage in the forest. After laying about four large eggs, the female takes no part in raising the chicks.

MALE

The male incubates the eggs by sitting on them for nearly two months. He then protects the brown and white striped chicks when they hatch. This is similar behaviour that occurs in emus and ostriches, birds that are related to the cassowary.

A cassowary nest is a simple hollow, scratched into the ground and lined with leaves.

WHAT THEY EAT

OMNIVORES

Cassowaries are omnivores, which means that they eat a wide variety of foods. Their diet is mostly fruits and seeds, but they also eat insects, and even small animals like frogs and lizards. They will catch and eat a small animal if they happen to come across it, but they do not seem to purposefully hunt other animals for food.

Cassowaries will raid garbage bins on farms and at camp sites, so always ensure rubbish in these areas is cleared away.

Cassowaries in captivity need to be kept away from areas where people might throw them food, since they will eat just about anything, no matter how unhealthy it is for them.

FRUIT AND SEEDS

As fruit eaters, cassowaries are one of the important spreaders of seeds in the rainforest, contributing to the growth of trees and bushes, and helping to maintain the rainforest diversity. Cassowaries cannot live on open grassland like emus do because of the different diets both of these birds have.

PREDATORS

Packs of feral dogs are a main predator of cassowaries, whose natural defences are not enough to allow them to defend themselves and their chicks against an attack. Feral pigs will also attack and eat the chicks or the eggs.

HABITAT LOSS

The loss of rainforests through logging, bushfires and clearing are having a negative effect on the southern cassowary in Australia.

ROADKILL

Being killed by motor vehicles is as much a threat to cassowaries as it is to other wildlife in Australia. Since the male is the parent that cares for the chicks, if he is killed then his young chicks will have little chance of survival.

There are only a few thousand southern cassowaries left in the wild, and their numbers are not stable.

Cassowary breeding programs are underway in zoos in Australia and overseas.

CASSOWARIES AND PEOPLE

Southern cassowaries and people do not get on well. Cassowaries are large, heavy and aggressive, so move away if you happen to encounter one in the rainforest. Their excellent senses will have told them you are there long before you can see them.

TERRITORIES

Male and female southern cassowaries both lay claim to large territories. The female's claim is larger and can be over a square kilometre. If you are intruding on her patch, expect trouble.

CHICKS

Although the chicks look cute, don't assume a chick you see in the rainforest is lost or orphaned. The father cassowary is likely to be nearby and will attack you if you go anywhere near his chicks.

FEEDING

As with all native wildlife in Australia, never feed cassowaries. This encourages them to seek out humans for handouts of food, a situation that can easily go wrong and lead to a dangerous outcome.

It is illegal to feed cassowaries in Queensland. It is for their safety and ours.

WHERE TO SEE A CASSOWARY

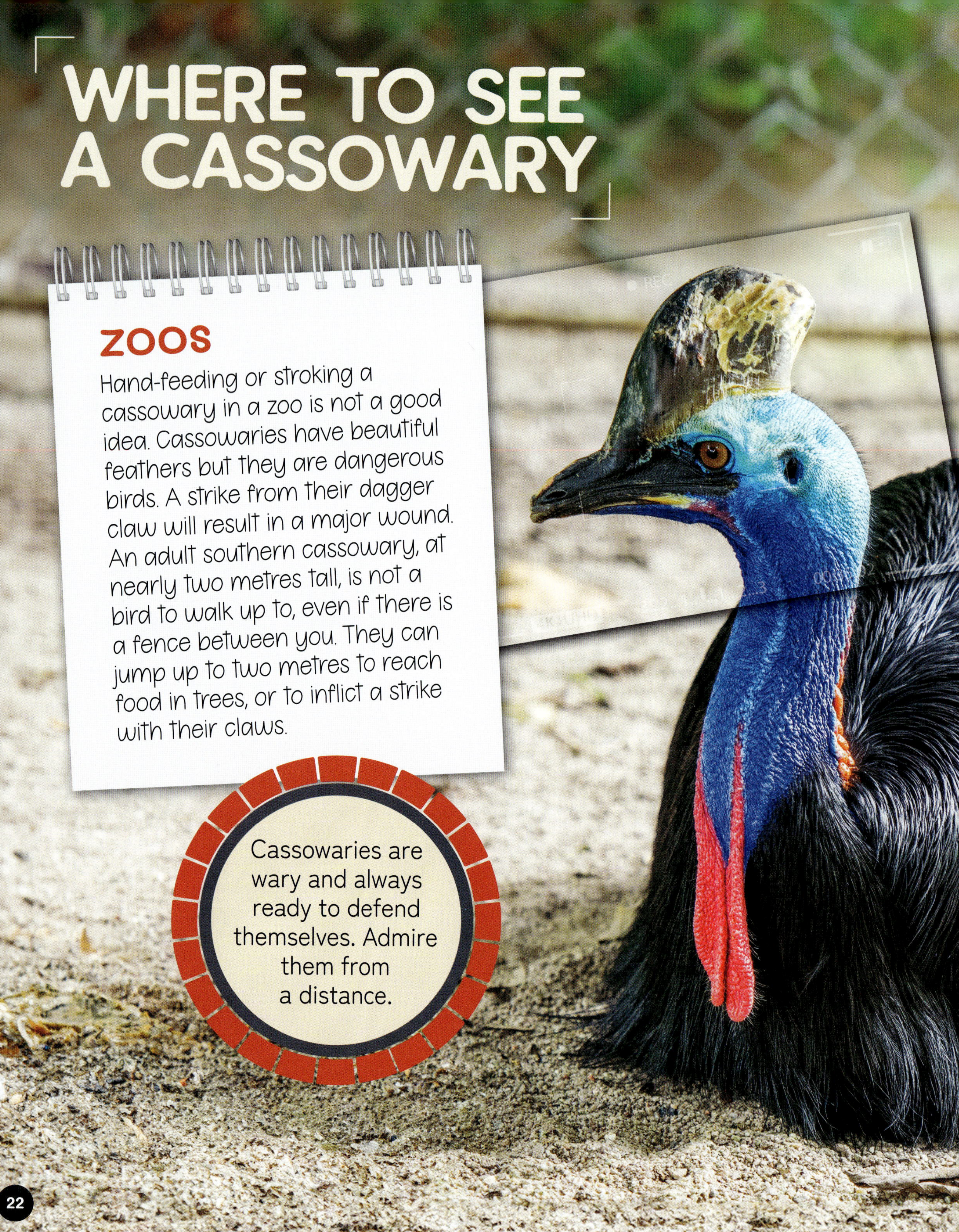

ZOOS

Hand-feeding or stroking a cassowary in a zoo is not a good idea. Cassowaries have beautiful feathers but they are dangerous birds. A strike from their dagger claw will result in a major wound. An adult southern cassowary, at nearly two metres tall, is not a bird to walk up to, even if there is a fence between you. They can jump up to two metres to reach food in trees, or to inflict a strike with their claws.

Cassowaries are wary and always ready to defend themselves. Admire them from a distance.

IN THE WILD

It is rare to see a southern cassowary in the wild in a rainforest for two reasons. Firstly, they are decreasing in numbers, and secondly, they can sense you from a distance so will probably be hiding from you.

FARMLAND

As their rainforest habitat decreases, cassowaries sometimes go onto farmland in search of food.

DO THEY MAKE GOOD PETS?

NO!

Cassowaries are about as far from being good as pets as you could get!

It is illegal in Australia to keep a native animal as a pet. Wildlife carers need special government licensing to be allowed to look after sick and injured wildlife.

Cassowaries become aggressive as they mature. The growing cassowary will attack and drive off other cassowaries, as well as any humans nearby.

CHICKS

Although a cassowary chick will instinctively follow the first moving animal it sees when it breaks out of its green egg, it will lose this interest when it grows up.

Cassowaries are wild animals and cannot be domesticated. They may learn to seek food from humans who feed them, but they remain very unpredictable.

As a solitary animal, an adult cassowary does not have the social behaviour that would make it want to form a long-term bond with people.

OTHER RATITES

GONDWANA BREAKS UP

All of the five types of ratites living now evolved on the ancient continent Gondwana. This broke apart millions of years ago to form some of the landmasses we know today, including Australia.

FLIGHT

Ratites have all lost the ability to fly. They do not have the special feathers, bones and muscles needed for flight, but they make up for that loss by having long, strong legs and sharp claws. Even the fluffy, little kiwi will scratch if cornered.

All ratites have a dense covering of thin feathers that are useless for flying.

MOST DANGEROUS BIRD IN THE WORLD?

The cassowary is often called the most dangerous bird in the world, because of its aggressive attacks on people and any other living thing that comes near it.

If you find yourself in the rainforest facing a cassowary, slowly move away behind a tree. Don't run!

Although the beak and casque look menacing, it is the long dagger claws that you need to avoid!

The African ostrich, which is a relative of the Australian cassowary, is just as aggressive and more dangerous. Many more attacks on people are reported each year by the ostrich than the cassowary.

The reason the cassowary still retains the title as the most dangerous bird is possibly more related to the way it hides in the rainforest, suddenly appearing without any noise, ready to attack.

The cassowary prefers to be alone in the forest and does not hunt or seek out people to attack. It will respond immediately though if it feels threatened.

SORTING ANIMALS INTO GROUPS

Biologists divide all living things around the world into groups. They call this process classification. The two basic groups of animals are called:

INVERTEBRATES
Invertebrates do not have a backbone

VERTEBRATES
Vertebrates have a backbone

Vertebrates are further divided into five groups called classes. Humans are in the class called Mammalia.

FISH

MAMMALS (MAMMALIA)

BIRDS (AVES)
Cassowaries are birds and belong in the class called Aves.

AMPHIBIANS (AMPHIBIA)

REPTILES (REPTILIA)

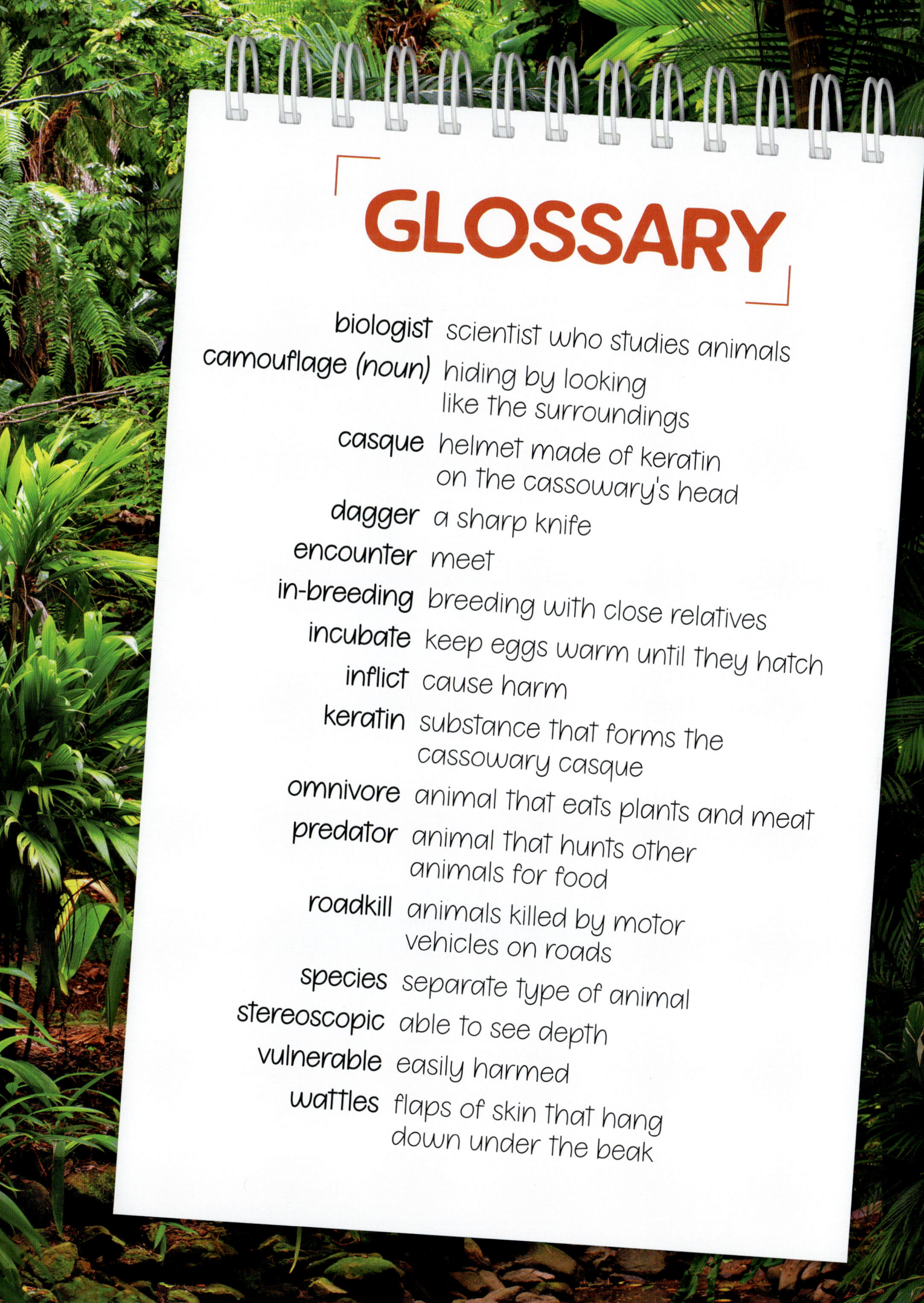

GLOSSARY

biologist scientist who studies animals

camouflage (noun) hiding by looking like the surroundings

casque helmet made of keratin on the cassowary's head

dagger a sharp knife

encounter meet

in-breeding breeding with close relatives

incubate keep eggs warm until they hatch

inflict cause harm

keratin substance that forms the cassowary casque

omnivore animal that eats plants and meat

predator animal that hunts other animals for food

roadkill animals killed by motor vehicles on roads

species separate type of animal

stereoscopic able to see depth

vulnerable easily harmed

wattles flaps of skin that hang down under the beak

INDEX